RUM MADE
ME DO IT

RUM MADE
ME DO IT

60 TANTALIZINGLY
TROPICAL COCKTAILS

LANCE J. MAYHEW
ILLUSTRATED BY RUBY TAYLOR

Andrews McMeel
PUBLISHING®

Andrews McMeel Publishing
A division of Andrews McMeel Universal
1130 Walnut Street, Kansas City, Missouri 64106

www.andrewsmcmeel.com

23 24 25 26 27 HPL 10 9 8 7 6 5 4 3 2 1

ISBN: 978-1-5248-8450-5

Library of Congress Control Number: 2022951262

ATTENTION: SCHOOLS AND BUSINESSES

Andrews McMeel books are available at quantity discounts with bulk purchase for educational, business, or sales promotional use. For information, please email the Andrews McMeel Publishing Special Sales Department: specialsales@amuniversal.com.

DISCLAIMER:

This book features recipes that include the optional use of raw eggs. Consuming raw eggs may increase the risk of food-borne illness. Individuals who are immunocompromised, pregnant, or elderly should use caution. Ensure eggs are fresh and meet local food-standard requirements.

Please drink responsibly.

CONTENTS

AN INTRODUCTION TO RUM

Kill-devil, rumbullion, *aguardiente*, grog, Barbados water—these are just a few of the names by which rum has been known throughout its long history. Rum has come a long way from its earliest incarnations, but even so, modern rums wouldn't seem too far removed from their original forms. In the end, rum is simply a spirit made from sugar (sugar cane, to be more exact), which is produced all over the world. Rum is found both in sugar-cane-growing regions as well as completely unexpected places—for instance, the team behind the wonderful Edinburgh cocktail bar, Bramble, distilled a white rum in Scotland in 2016. Because of the lack of geographic limitations for rum—unlike Scotch whisky that is from Scotland, tequila from Mexico, and so on—it is often stated that rum is the spirit category without rules. In a general sense that is correct, as the rules for rum can and do change from place to place, but the one constant requirement in all regulations for rum production is that the base source for the alcohol must come from sugar cane. From there, all bets are off.

WHAT IS RUM?

The French Caribbean, with its rhum agricole (the "h" in rhum is silent), specifies that freshly pressed cane juice must be used. Most other rum is made from molasses; some is made from skimmings from the sugar-making process itself. The type of still used to make rum varies, too; it can be a pot still, which results usually in a fuller-bodied and more flavorful rum, or a column still, which creates a lighter and crisper style. Even the type of material the still is made from can affect the final product—the equipment can be made from everything from clay and bamboo (perhaps the earliest distilling technology and yet still in use today) to stainless-steel or copper in modern distilleries, to the double-wooden pot still and wooden coffey used even today in Guyana for El Dorado rums.

Let us not forget maturation, either. Is the rum going to go straight from the still to bottling? Or perhaps it will be kept in open-top vats to allow some air flow and time to work their magic on the white rum before bottling? Perhaps the rum is destined to spend time in a used bourbon barrel or some other wooden container that may or may not add characteristics of the wood to the final product? All of these variables and more make the world of rum both utterly fascinating to enthusiasts who can spend an entire lifetime exploring the different varieties and flavors available. To the novice rum drinker, though, these same differences that make rum so varied can also present a bit of a challenge to understanding the spirit.

THE HISTORY OF RUM

Once known as the favored tipple of pirates and the British Navy, the story of rum has always been intertwined with the production of sugar and sugar cane. Contrary to what many people assume, rum wasn't first distilled in the Caribbean. In fact, by the time sugar cane reached the New World and rum started being distilled in the Caribbean and Latin America, it was already a very old spirit by any standard.

The earliest records of rum appear from an Indian historian who noted "arrack" was being traded in the Sultanate of Delhi in the fourteenth century. This early form of rum was made from either fresh sugar cane juice or a combination of sugar cane juice and raw sugar, and it was often flavored with spices and botanicals. These early distilled spirits would be recognizable as rum even today, and these flavored arrack were the first incarnation of what is now called spiced rum (predating brands like Captain Morgan and Sailor Jerry by several hundred years).

It was the Spanish who brought sugar cane to the New World via Christopher Columbus, on his second voyage to the region, and had it growing on the island of Hispaniola (modern-day Haiti and the Dominican Republic) by 1500. The Portuguese introduced sugar cane to Brazil in 1520, the first time this crop was grown on the South American continent. Prior to this, the Spanish and Portuguese had sugar cane growing in places like the Canary Islands, Madeira, and the Cape Verde islands, so this was more of a shift and expansion in production to the New World, where growing conditions for sugar cane were better and as a result yields were larger. Not long after the Spanish and Portuguese, the English, French, and Dutch also began to colonize and vie for power in the New World. During that time the notorious triangle trade of slaves for molasses for rum began, as English colonies from New England to the Caribbean started to make rum from molasses. With colonization and the push to grow sugar cane in the New World came rum distillation as a natural byproduct of the sugar industry.

In the 1600s, the Viceroy of New España (New Spain), now modern Mexico, banned distilling in general and particularly those from cane sugar or cane juice. In the same approximate period of time, Brazil, under the auspices of the Portuguese, banned distilling from cane. Neither effort was effective, but it does show us how quickly cane spirits came to be distilled in the New World after the introduction of sugar cane. By the middle of the 1600s, a Cuban official noted two forms of *aguardiente* (fire water) available on the island. One made from the skimmings of the rum-making process called *cachaza* and the other, less popular, made from freshly pressed cane juice.

While distillation of cane spirits was widespread in Latin America, it's when their distillation reached the Caribbean, notably in the British colony of Barbados and the French colony of Martinique, that rum became a profitable item and the subject of international trade. It was during this period that the term rum became commonly used for cane spirits, and the British Navy began issuing rum to select sailors, before making it an official part of the sailors' ration in the 1700s.

Rum became an international commodity by the 1700s, with rum (and molasses) being shipped up to New England, which ran its own distilleries for making rum, in addition to its imported rum. Across the Atlantic, rum exports were reaching the shores of Ireland and it was even traded on the Central and West African coasts, where it became a key item in gifting ceremonies before trade negotiations. As rum exports grew and demand increased, rum distilleries in the Caribbean increased their output. At the same time, several European powers, including Spain and France, did all they could to stamp out the rum industry and protect their native wine and brandy industries.

THE RISE OF THE RUM DISTILLERY

The 1800s brought the Industrial Revolution to the world, and with it changes to distilling technology in the form of the column still. While many other distillers adopted this method to increase their yields, the rum industry was slow to move past pot still distillation, instead purchasing larger pot stills or adding "doublers" (an addition to a pot still that creates a final product that is similar to something that has been double distilled in pot stills). This, along with a worldwide crash in sugar prices brought on by sugar beets being subsidized for sugar production by European countries, led to consolidation in sugar cane production. Then, a terrible thing happened to the wine industry that helped revive the flagging rum distillers—phylloxera. This root louse devastated European vineyards in the middle of the 1800s, vastly reducing both European wine and brandy production, leading European nations to open their markets to rum again and to their citizens developing a taste for rum. This was also the time of the expansion of the sugar industry into Cuba, and by the latter half of the 1800s one Facundo Bacardi started a distillery with support from his brother, and found the United States market to be quite fond of Cuban rums. Puerto Rico was ceded to the United States in

1898 and it too was quickly planted with sugar cane, which marked the beginning of the Puerto Rican rum industry.

By the tail end of the 1800s, the iconic daiquiri was created—a simple combination of rum, lime, and sugar that became even more popular in places like Havana once American Prohibition started in 1920. The Prohibition period (1920–33) brought Americans south to places like Cuba and Mexico where rum flowed freely, helping the American public further their enjoyment of rum. By the middle of the twentieth century, Cuba and Puerto Rico were the two dominant rum producers in the world, both using column still distillation to produce crisp, light rums that were becoming increasingly popular with the public. The Cuban Revolution in 1959 closed the door on Cuban rum to the American market, and the end of the Colonial era meant that many distilleries in the Caribbean and elsewhere now had to take on their own marketing and sales in addition to distilling. More and more distillers continued to invest in column stills to deliver the crisper, white rum style that was in demand while more full-flavored rums struggled to gain commercial success beyond their home markets.

Luckily for rum, two men, Ernest Raymond Gantt (better known as Donn Beach) and Victor Bergeron (who adopted the *nom de guerre* Trader Vic) helped usher in the Polynesian tiki bar craze in the United States after World War II. These men developed the subset of cocktails that came to be known as tiki drinks. Colorful creations served in exotic glassware, these drinks of Donn Beach and Trader Vic often relied on flavorful Caribbean rums mixed with fresh juices and rich syrups to create delicious, boozy concoctions with fanciful origination stories. While tiki bars began in the 1930s, they had a successful run in the United States up into the 1970s, creating an essential lifeline of business for less-favored styles of rum.

Fast forward to the twenty-first century and bartenders have rediscovered rum, and with it a love for rum-based cocktails. From complex tiki drinks to classics like the daiquiri, to lesser-known drinks like the Corn 'N' Oil, rum and its many variations has made a comeback in the spirits world and now accounts for more than 10% of spirits sales worldwide.

PRODUCTION

Before we journey too far down rum's definition, though, let's address rums that aren't made from sugar cane. Table sugar can be produced from the sugar beet as well as sugar cane, and if you look hard enough, you'll come across rum distilled from a sugar-beet base instead of sugar cane. You might even find a rum distilled from sorghum, which is a grain. However, if you look to the rules and definitions of rum from the EU, USA, Brazil, Cuba, or CARICOM (the Caribbean community), all state that sugar cane must be the base of all rum. How products get labeled as rum when they are made from sugar beets or sorghum or another base is an issue for another book, but for this one, we'll stick to sugar cane-based rums that constitute both the vast majority of rums produced worldwide and the only truly authentic rums.

There are a few more components that are important for producing a good-quality rum:

Yeast is essential for any distilled product, and the breadth and depth of yeasts used in rum production runs the gamut from regular bakers' yeast to champagne yeasts to exotic yeasts cultivated specifically to provide specific flavors to the final product. This is one of the first steps in distilling, as yeast and warm water are added to molasses (or fresh cane juice) to begin the fermentation of sugars into alcohol.

Water is also essential to rum distilling. There is a saying that good water makes good rum, and the pH of a particular water source also adds a unique fingerprint to the final rum that could not be replicated even if the distillery was moved to a different location.

Maturation involves the interaction of the spirit with oxygen and often the wood of a barrel. Freshly distilled rum that goes straight into the bottle will be crisper than a rum that has had exposure to oxygen for a period of time. Wood adds an additional influence, with flavors and tannins being introduced to the maturing spirit as well as evaporation (frequently called the "Angel's Share"), which concentrates the flavors in the barrel.

Climate, specifically the ambient temperature and humidity, plays a major role in the flavors that rums can have. To start, fermentation in warmer temperatures allows yeasts to produce fruitier esters, which find their way into the final product. Additionally, the tropical climate in sugar-cane-growing regions mean that the "Angel's Share" or amount lost to evaporation can be much higher than, say, in Scotch whisky, which matures in a much cooler climate. Because of this rapid evaporation, rum can mature much more quickly than spirits in cooler climates and occasionally entire barrels can be lost to evaporation if left too long or if they are forgotten in the corner of a warehouse. As a general rule of thumb, one year of aging for a rum from a tropical climate is the equivalent of three years of aging of a spirit in a cooler climate.

Stills, both the pot still and the column still and their variants, are used in rum distillation. The pot still is an older and less efficient style of distillation. Modern stills are heated by steam, although older stills are still heated by fire. Pot stills work in batches, and the design of the pot still itself will also contribute to the flavor. A shorter still with a short neck produces a more full-flavored rum, while a taller pot still with a longer neck will result in a milder rum. As it's a more inefficient process than a column still, more of the original base fermentation comes through the distillation, with a pot still being capable of producing a spirit of 40–80% ABV per distillation.

RUM STYLES

To make the world of rum a bit more accessible, let us look first at the styles of rum generally produced in the areas that were colonized by various countries, and then we will give a general breakdown of rum categories. One important caveat to note: these are very general rules of thumb for rum; exceptions can and do exist for almost all of these categories, but the information here is hopefully helpful in narrowing down the world of rum to a more manageable size. Finally, we'll explore the general styles of rum available.

First, let us look at rum (or rhum) produced in areas colonized by the English, French, and Spanish, which are primarily islands in the Caribbean. Originally, the distilleries on these islands would have been used to provision local ships and residents, but as the colonizers developed a taste for rum on the islands, it created a demand for the spirit when they began to return to their home countries.

English-style rums tend toward using either pot still or a combination of pot still and column still rums. These rums are generally medium to full-bodied. English-style rums are usually made from molasses. Countries famous for English-style rums include Jamaica, Guyana, Barbados, Antigua, and Guyana.

Spanish-style rums (often labeled as "*ron*," the Spanish word for rum) are a contrast to English-style rums as they frequently favor column stills, which result in a lighter, crisper style of rum. Spanish-style rums are usually made from molasses and are produced in Cuba, Puerto Rico, Panama, Nicaragua, the Dominican Republic, Costa Rica, Ecuador, and Mexico.

French-style rums are better known as rhum agricole. These are rhums produced from fresh sugar cane juice versus the molasses base usually found in other rum styles. The end result is a funkier, grassier note to the rum that many rhum enthusiasts swoon over, whether drinking neat or in cocktails. It's worth noting that rum can also be produced in places that produce rhum agricole, but if labeled as rum it would be a molasses base. Martinique and Guadeloupe are home to well-regarded rhum agricole distilleries as well as Haiti, Réunion, and Mauritius.

So where did the Dutch go in all of this? How come there aren't Dutch-style rums? There certainly are distilleries on islands in the Caribbean and Latin America that are colonized by the Dutch, and even rums (or, more properly, arrack) from former Dutch colonies in Southeast Asia like Java, but there isn't a common style that would indicate a Dutch rum, unlike the English, Spanish, and French styles. Saint Martin and Java are home to rum distilleries with Dutch heritage.

Second, let's look at general styles of rum. Again, these are categories that should be used as rules of thumb, but expect exceptions to the rule. However, if you use this in combination with the above list of styles by colonial power, it's easier to figure out that a white rum from Jamaica (a former British colony) is likely to be fuller-bodied and richer than, say, a white rum from Cuba (a former colony of Spain).

White rum is essentially any rum that comes as a clear spirit. **Silver** or **Platinum** are other monikers used to describe this category. Most white rums from major brands are going to be distilled on a column still (think Bacardi), giving them a clean, crisp flavor that makes them eminently mixable. Occasionally, you may run across a pure pot still rum (Wray & Nephew from Jamaica is a fine example). These pot still rums will be more flavorful, with notes of vanilla and fruits apparent. Then there are white rums that try to find the happy medium with a combination of pot still and column still rums blended together. Lastly, there are white rums that have been matured in barrels and then have had the color stripped out via filtration. These rums are often referred to as cristallino or cristal on their labels.

Gold rums have been matured in a barrel for some time. While a darker color is often indicative of additional age, it isn't always the case. Some rum distillers use caramel to color correct their batches for consistency, but the use of caramel can also introduce a darker color to the rum. Further, the age of the barrel and how many times it has been filled and refilled also affects the amount of wood maturation that an individual barrel contributes to color and flavor. A first-use barrel contributes a lot of color and flavor to the wood, a first refill less so, a second refill even less, and the third refill is almost imperceptible. Most distillers accept that by the fourth time a barrel is reused and refilled without being retoasted, the container essentially becomes inert and little to no wood influence is contributed to the rum.

Dark rum, sometimes referred to as **black rum**, is matured for a longer period of time than a gold rum and may be matured in a more heavily charred cask. Some distillers will use caramel to artificially darken a rum. You can tell a genuine dark rum based on its mouthfeel—it should feel very dry from the presence of wood tannins imbued into the spirit over time from the barrel maturation.

Navy strength rum has its origins in the British Naval tradition of serving grog (a combination of rum, lime juice, and water) in the 1700s. As the navy sailed around to various places, water and its potability were an issue, as well as the threat of scurvy (caused by a deficiency of vitamin C in the diet). When the British Navy would arrive in a new port, they would look to buy barrels of rum. A small amount of rum would be placed in a spoon and if it ignited (50% ABV or more will flame), it was "proof" that the rum was good for purchase. This also led to the term proof being used to express the alcoholic content in spirits (proof being twice the alcoholic strength by volume, so 40% ABV is 80 proof).

These days, the British Navy is dry, having done away with their daily rum ration on July 31, 1970, a day known as Black Tot Day. In modern times, navy-strength rums are often a blend of rums and are bottled at a high alcohol by volume percentage.

Spiced rum often gets a bad rap from rum enthusiasts, but rum has had flavorings added to enhance the taste from the earliest days of distillation. While modern spiced rum really took off in the 1980s, often being mixed with cola, these rums have a variety of flavor profiles, often with vanilla, cinnamon, and baking spices dominating.

Solera rum is a concept that was first used in Spain for sherry maturation. The goal of a solera system is to create a consistent and quality rum by blending older rums with younger ones. Imagine, if you will, an upside-down pyramid of barrels—ten barrels on top narrowing down to one at the bottom. At the top the ten barrels are filled with new-make rum. The row below that holds slightly older rum, and so on as you move down. The bottom barrel is where the rum is drawn off. When it is time to refill the bottom barrel, the barrels in the row above it are used to fill it, then those are refilled from the barrels above them, and so on until the top row of barrels is topped off with more new-make rum. In theory, this constant intermingling of newer and older distillates creates a richer, more flavorful profile as the solera continues to age. These make for very interesting rums and are worth seeking out.

Demerara rums are produced in Guyana and are blends of distillates aged in barrels at high humidity and temperatures, giving a smokiness that is unique to these rums. If you can't locate a Demerara rum for a recipe, substitute a Jamaican rum, as they are closest in style and taste.

Rhum agricole is made from freshly pressed sugar cane juice, as discussed on page 14. While rhum is made throughout the Caribbean, Martinique rhums are made under certain production standards to use the French-protected AOC (appellation d'origine contrôlée) "AOC Rhum Agricole Martinique." Guadeloupe is also considered one of the finest producers of rhum agricole, although rhum from Guadeloupe does not have a French AOC designation.

Cachaça is similar to rhum agricole in that it is produced from freshly pressed sugar cane juice, but it is only produced in Brazil, where it is the most popular spirit in the country. Essential to making a caipirinha, cachaça comes in white, gold, or aged varieties—the white is generally favored for making cocktails while the aged varieties are preferred neat.

SYRUPS

SIMPLE SYRUP
Add 1 cup of sugar to a small pan and pour in 8 fluid ounces of water. Set over medium heat and stir occasionally until the sugar dissolves. Remove from the heat and let it cool. Store the syrup in an airtight container in the refrigerator for up to one week.

BROWN SUGAR SIMPLE SYRUP
Add 1 cup of brown sugar to a small pan and pour in 8 fluid ounces of water. Set over medium heat and stir occasionally until the sugar dissolves. Remove from the heat and let it cool. Store the syrup in an airtight container in the refrigerator for up to one week.

RICH DEMERARA SIMPLE SYRUP
Add 1 cup of demerara sugar to a small pan and pour in 8 fluid ounces of water. Set over medium heat and stir occasionally until the sugar dissolves. Remove from the heat and let it cool. Store the syrup in an airtight container in the refrigerator for up to one week.

PASSIONFRUIT SIMPLE SYRUP

Add 1 cup of sugar to a small pan and pour in 8 fluid ounces of water. Set over medium heat and stir occasionally until the sugar dissolves. Remove from the heat and let it cool. Slice 4 passionfruit in half and scoop the pulp into the syrup. Let the fruit steep in the syrup for 2 hours. Set a fine-mesh sieve over a glass measuring jug with a spout and pour the contents of the pan into the sieve. To avoid a cloudy simple syrup, don't press on the solids, just let the syrup drain naturally into the measuring jug. Transfer to an airtight container and store in the refrigerator for up to one week.

CINNAMON SIMPLE SYRUP

Add 2 cinnamon sticks to the basic Simple Syrup recipe (see opposite page), after the sugar has dissolved, and allow the cinnamon to infuse the syrup for 20 minutes before transferring to an airtight container and storing in the refrigerator for up to one week.

HONEY SIMPLE SYRUP

Combine 2 parts honey with 1 part water, which helps the thick sweetener dissolve into cold cocktails. Make as much as you like, stirring to an even consistency. Store in an airtight container in the refrigerator for up to two weeks.

THE RECIPES

SPANISH COFFEE

Order up a Spanish Coffee in Spain and you'll likely be served a Carajillo (see page 24). In the United States, though, a Spanish Coffee is often a tableside show. In this performance, a 151 proof rum is flamed with triple sec to caramelize a sugared rim before freshly brewed coffee is added, and then the drink is finished with a dollop of fresh whipped cream. Huber's, the oldest restaurant in Portland, Oregon, is famous for its flaming Spanish Coffee, making it a popular stop for locals and tourists looking to experience this modern classic.

Ingredients
a lemon wedge, to garnish
superfine sugar, for decorating the glass
¾ fluid ounce 151 proof rum
¼ fluid ounce triple sec
1 ½ fluid ounces coffee liqueur
3 fluid ounces freshly brewed coffee
whipped cream, to garnish
ground cinnamon and grated nutmeg, to garnish (optional)

Instructions
Coat the rim of an Irish coffee mug by running a lemon wedge around it, then dip it into a shallow dish of superfine sugar. Add the 151 proof rum and triple sec to the mug. Carefully ignite the spirits and slowly rotate the flaming spirits by turning the mug to caramelize the sugar on the rim and heat the mug. Add the coffee liqueur (the flame will likely go out at this point) and top up with the fresh coffee. Gently spoon the freshly whipped cream onto the surface of the coffee to garnish, and if you like, add a dusting of ground cinnamon and/or grated nutmeg.

Tip: It's important to temper your mug if you are using a glass one— filling it with hot water and letting it sit for 30 seconds before pouring out the water will suffice. Forgetting to do this can result in the mug cracking or breaking when you flame the rum.

CARAJILLO

A Carajillo (or its close cousin the Belmonte) is often ordered in Spain at the end of a meal, especially when you're heading out to enjoy the nightlife afterwards. A simple DIY cocktail made with rum (or occasionally brandy), espresso, and perhaps a bit of sugar for sweetness, this drink transforms into the Belmonte when you add cream according to the drinker's preference.

Ingredients
freshly brewed espresso coffee
a bottle of rum
superfine sugar
cream (optional)

Instructions
Put a full shot of espresso into an espresso glass or demitasse cup. Place a bottle of rum next to the espresso with a bowl of sugar. Add rum and sugar to taste, and some cream, if you like. Offer up a hearty *Salud!* and enjoy.

RUM OLD FASHIONED

While the Old Fashioned is traditionally made with whiskey, a Rum Old Fashioned is utterly delicious as well, and it's a fun addition to any mixologist's repertoire. Use this recipe as a starting point for finding your perfect Rum Old Fashioned. Feel free to play with the type of bitters used, the type of rum, or even the type of sugar. While the combinations are endless, the results are uniformly delicious.

Ingredients

2 fluid ounces rum
4 dashes of orange bitters
4 dashes of Angostura bitters
½ fluid ounce Brown Sugar Simple Syrup (see page 18)
an orange peel twist and a cherry, to garnish

Instructions

Add the rum, bitters, and Brown Sugar Simple Syrup to an old fashioned glass. Add some ice—don't fill the glass, add one large cube or just add enough ice to half-fill it—then stir to combine the ingredients. Garnish with an orange twist expressed over the surface of the drink. Drop the twist into the drink and garnish with a cherry.

Tip: Just about any rum should work well here, but for best results avoid spiced rums and white rums.

PINEAPPLE FIZZ

The Pineapple Fizz isn't well known in modern times, but this is an easy drink that's really worth discovering. Originally appearing in famed London barman Harry Craddock's *The Savoy Cocktail Book* (1930), we've updated this cocktail with the addition of lime juice to create a refreshing long drink that is perfect for warm summer evenings.

Ingredients
2 fluid ounces white rum
½ fluid ounce lime juice
1 fluid ounce pineapple juice
½ fluid ounce Simple Syrup (see page 18)
club soda, to top up
a pineapple wedge, to garnish

Instructions
In a cocktail shaker, combine the first four ingredients and add some ice. Shake vigorously and strain into an ice-filled highball glass. Top up the glass with club soda and garnish with a pineapple wedge.

RUM COLLINS

The Collins family is unusual in that many of the variations of this drink are known by men's names. The Tom Collins is gin-based, the John Collins has whiskey in it, and even the Juan Collins calls for a tequila base. Somehow the Rum Collins never got a first name assigned to it, but it is the finest version of the entire Collins family. Even James Bond agrees, with the iconic spy enjoying a Rum Collins in 1965's *Thunderball*.

Ingredients
2 fluid ounces rum
1 fluid ounce lime juice
½ fluid ounce Simple Syrup (see page 18)
club soda, to top up
a lemon wheel and a cherry, to garnish

Instructions
Add the rum, lime juice, and Simple Syrup to a Collins glass. Add ice to the glass and top up with club soda. Give the drink a quick stir with a bar spoon to incorporate the ingredients. Garnish with a lemon wheel and a cherry.

RUM SOUR

Sours are one of the original families of cocktail drinks and are still extremely popular today. The first reference in print was in Jerry Thomas' seminal cocktail book of 1862, *How to Mix Drinks*, or *The Bon Vivant's Companion*, although the drink family was long established before this. While white rums provide a clean, crisp profile, try a rum with some age on it for a richer, fuller experience. To change things up, try straining the drink into a chilled martini glass instead of over ice for an elegant dinner party presentation.

Ingredients
2 fluid ounces rum (any will do, but darker
    rums shine in this cocktail)
1 ½ fluid ounces lemon juice
1 fluid ounce Simple Syrup (see page 18)
1 egg white (optional)
a cherry, to garnish

Instructions
Add the rum, lemon juice, and Simple Syrup to a cocktail shaker filled with ice. Shake vigorously for 30 seconds, then strain into a clean glass. For a fluffier cocktail, add an egg white—discard the ice and pour the cocktail back into the shaker, then add the egg white and shake well for 30 seconds or so (dry shaking like this will help the egg white foam up to form a fluffy topping). Pour into an old fashioned glass filled with ice and garnish with a cherry.

HOT GROG (RUM TODDY)

Grog conjures up images of pirates and sailors drinking rum with a bit of citrus to avoid scurvy during long voyages. This Hot Grog takes that concept and turns it into the perfect warmer for the coldest nights of winter. A gold or aged rum will work best, but a spiced rum can be a surprising revelation in this drink as well.

Ingredients

2 fluid ounces rum (for a more authentic grog experience use an overproof or Navy-strength rum)

½ fluid ounce honey

1 tea bag (Earl Grey recommended but any non-herbal tea will do)

½ lemon wheel studded with 4–6 cloves, to garnish

Instructions

Add the rum, honey, and tea bag to a heatproof glass and top up with just-boiled water. Stir briefly to combine and leave to steep for 3 minutes. Squeeze the lemon wheel into the drink, then drop the wheel into the cocktail.

XYZ COCKTAIL

The XYZ is a 1920s' riff on the classic Sidecar, the more popular brandy-based version of this cocktail. With just three ingredients—rum, triple sec, and lemon juice—this is as easy to prepare as it is delicious. Feel free to play with different styles of rum here to find your favorite variation; a rhum from Martinique is going to add a funky complexity, while a white Puerto Rican rum will yield a clean and crisp cocktail.

Ingredients
2 fluid ounces rum
1 fluid ounce triple sec (Cointreau if you can)
1 fluid ounce lemon juice
a nosegay of mint and a cherry, to garnish

Instructions
In a cocktail shaker, combine all the ingredients with some ice and shake vigorously. Strain the drink over ice (or a large ice cube) into an old fashioned glass. Garnish with a nosegay of mint and a cherry.

PAULINE COCKTAIL

Who is Pauline? No one seems to know, but adding a small amount of absinthe to a rum and lemon cocktail creates an herbal complexity. If you find the ¼ fluid ounce of absinthe to be a bit too strong, instead simply rinse the martini glass with a small amount of absinthe, then dump anything that doesn't coat the glass before straining the rest of the cocktail into the glass.

Ingredients
2 fluid ounces light rum
1 fluid ounce lemon juice
1 fluid ounce Simple Syrup (see page 18)
¼ fluid ounce absinthe

Instructions
In a cocktail shaker, combine all the ingredients with some ice. Shake vigorously and strain into a martini glass.

RUM DAISY

The Daisy is a very old style of drink that has many variations which make it hard to tell what is actually a Daisy. Originally made with brandy, lemon, and triple sec, it has evolved over time to a base spirit, citrus, and then a liqueur or cordial. Yellow chartreuse lends its subtle herbal sweetness well to a pairing of aged rum and lemon, creating a delightfully boozy and citrus-forward aperitif.

Ingredients
2 fluid ounces Añejo rum
¼ fluid ounce yellow chartreuse
¾ fluid ounce lemon juice
½ fluid ounce Simple Syrup (see page 18)
1–2 dashes of Angostura bitters
mint leaves and a cherry, to garnish

Instructions
In a cocktail shaker, combine all of the ingredients with some ice. Shake vigorously and strain into an old fashioned glass half-filled with ice or a large ice cube. Garnish with mint leaves and a cherry.

RUM RUNNER

This 1950s' creation from a Florida tiki bar called Holiday Isle has spawned countless variations that may or may not resemble the original cocktail. Traditionally, the Rum Runner combines multiple rums with fruit juice, banana liqueur, grenadine, and blackberry liqueur to create a potent concoction that is evocative of a tropical vacation.

Ingredients
1 fluid ounce white rum
1 fluid ounce overproof rum
1 fluid ounce banana liqueur
½ fluid ounce blackberry brandy
1½ fluid ounces pineapple juice
1½ fluid ounces orange juice
1 fluid ounce lime juice
½ fluid ounce grenadine
a cherry and pineapple wedge, to garnish

Instructions
In a cocktail shaker, combine all the ingredients with some ice. Shake vigorously and strain into an ice-filled hurricane glass. Garnish with a cherry and a pineapple wedge.

ORIGINAL MAI TAI

Although there is some dispute over who created the original Mai Tai (Donn Beach also claims to have mixed this drink under another name in the early 1930s), this original version of the Mai Tai was created at the Polynesian-themed Trader Vic's and is indisputably one of the finest rum drinks ever created.

Ingredients

2 fluid ounces aged rum
¾ fluid ounce lime juice
½ fluid ounce orange curaçao
½ fluid ounce orgeat syrup
¼ fluid ounce Rich Demerara Simple Syrup (see page 18)
a lime half and mint sprig, to garnish

Instructions

In a cocktail shaker, combine all of the ingredients with some ice. Shake vigorously and pour the entire contents (including the ice) into an old fashioned glass. Garnish with the lime half and a mint sprig.

ROYAL HAWAIIAN HOTEL MAI TAI

Walk into any bar and order a Mai Tai and chances are this (or a simpler version omitting the orgeat syrup and curaçao) is the version you'll get. In 1954, Trader Vic himself was hired to design the cocktail menus for two hotels in Hawaii. Needing a faster, simpler version of his famous Mai Tai, Trader Vic put together this variation, which has become the far more popular of the two recipes. Potent and flavorful, this Mai Tai is as easy to make at home as it is to order in a bar.

Ingredients
1 fluid ounce white rum
1 fluid ounce orange juice
2 fluid ounces pineapple juice
½ fluid ounce orgeat syrup
½ fluid ounce orange curaçao
float of dark rum (approximately ½–1 fluid ounce, to taste)
a pineapple wedge, lime wedge, and a cherry
    speared on a parasol, to garnish

Instructions
In a cocktail shaker, combine all of the ingredients, except the dark rum, with some ice. "Roll" the shaker in a circular motion several times and pour the entire contents (including ice) into an old fashioned glass. Using a bar spoon or cherry, float dark rum on the surface of the drink. Garnish with a pineapple wedge, a lime wedge, and a cherry speared on a parasol.

RUM SWIZZLE

The national drink of Bermuda, the Rum Swizzle is a potent combination of rum, fruit juices, and grenadine mixed by spinning a swizzle stick rapidly between one's hands until a thick frost appears on the outside of the glass. Swizzle sticks (a long, thin stick with horizontal prongs) are traditionally made from the branches of a tree native to the Caribbean, but most swizzle sticks now are made from plastic or metal. No matter what material, a good swizzle stick and Bermudan rums are the key to a great Rum Swizzle.

Ingredients
1 fluid ounce Goslings Black Seal Rum
1 fluid ounce Goslings Gold Seal Rum
2 fluid ounces orange juice
2 fluid ounces pineapple juice
¼ fluid ounce grenadine
2 dashes of Angostura bitters
a cherry, orange slice, and pineapple wedge, to garnish

Instructions
Fill an old fashioned glass halfway with ice and pour in all the ingredients. Vigorously "swizzle" the drink by rotating the stick or bar spoon back and forth between your hands until a thick frost appears on the outside of the glass. Top off with more ice to fill the glass. Garnish with a cherry, orange slice, and pineapple wedge.

TI PUNCH

This popular drink from the French Caribbean (Martinique and Guadeloupe) is traditionally served without ice, but feel free to add ice if you prefer. On the islands, there is a saying that translates to "each prepares his own death," as Ti Punch comes served on a tray with an empty glass, some cut limes, a bottle of local rhum, and a swizzle stick, and you prepare your own punch to your liking.

Ingredients
2 fluid ounces rhum agricole
½ fluid ounce cane syrup, or to taste
1 lime wedge, or to taste

Instructions
Pour the rhum agricole into a glass and add the cane syrup to taste. Squeeze and drop in the lime wedge to taste. Mix with a swizzle stick or spoon to combine. Add an ice cube or two if needed.

Tip: Use only a rhum made from fresh sugar cane juice for a proper Ti Punch. Do not substitute molasses-based rums as they lack the funky, vegetal character of rhum agricole.

RUM PUNCH

Sometimes you just need a quick and easy punch. A few rums, a mixture of fruit juices, a little citrus to add acidity, and a bit of grenadine for color. Think of this as the 101 class in making a rum punch; most of these ingredients can be substituted for something similar and you'll still get great results. Want it a little less boozy? Add ginger ale or lemon-lime soda to lengthen this drink.

Ingredients

1½ fluid ounces light rum
1½ fluid ounces dark rum
2 fluid ounces pineapple juice
½ fluid ounce lime juice
1 fluid ounce orange juice
¼ fluid ounce grenadine
a cherry, to garnish

Instructions

Add all the ingredients to a cocktail shaker. Fill with ice and shake vigorously. Strain into an ice-filled hurricane glass. Garnish with a cherry.

Make it a pitcher: Increase each ingredient in proportion to the number of servings needed. Break out the punch bowl and combine everything with some ice.

DAIQUIRI

While so many Daiquiris are served frozen, the classic Daiquiri is shaken and served up. Named after a Cuban mining town in the late nineteenth century, the Daiquiri was popularized when a US Navy medical officer brought the recipe home with him to Washington, DC. To make the frozen version of this drink, just add the ingredients to a blender with 1 cup of ice and blend on high for about 10 seconds.

Ingredients
2 fluid ounces light rum
1 fluid ounce lime juice
1 fluid ounce Simple Syrup (see page 18)
a lime wedge, to garnish

Instructions
Add all the ingredients to a cocktail shaker. Fill with ice and shake vigorously. Strain into a coupe or martini glass and garnish with a lime wedge.

HEMINGWAY DAIQUIRI

Ernest Hemingway may be as famous a drinker as he was a writer. The Hemingway Daiquiri he bragged about having created for him at Havana's El Floridita Bar didn't contain any sugar and had double the amount of alcohol of this version. Perhaps Papa Hemingway was more into quantity over quality, but the Hemingway Daiquiri here isn't quite as boozy and is much more drinkable than the original.

Ingredients
2 fluid ounces white rum
½ fluid ounce maraschino liqueur
¾ fluid ounce lime juice
1 fluid ounce grapefruit juice
¼ fluid ounce Simple Syrup (see page 18)
a lime wheel, to garnish

Instructions
In a cocktail shaker, combine all the ingredients with some ice. Shake vigorously and strain into a martini glass or coupe. Garnish with a lime wheel.

MOJITO

A traditional Cuban drink, Ernest Hemingway liked to drink his at La Bodeguita del Medio in Old Havana. Sloppy Joe's, another Havana bar a short walk from La Bodeguita, gets credit for the first recorded recipe for a Mojito in print, circa 1932. A five-ingredient cocktail of rum, sugar, lime, mint, and soda, this is both refreshing and utterly delicious on a hot day.

Ingredients
4–6 mint leaves, plus extra to garnish
½ fluid ounce Simple Syrup (see page 18)
2 fluid ounces white rum
1 fluid ounce lime juice
club soda, to top up
a lime wheel, to garnish

Instructions
Add the mint leaves and Simple Syrup to the bottom of your glass and muddle together to release the herb's essential oils. Add the rum, lime juice, and ice and top up with the club soda. Garnish with more mint leaves, slightly crushed to release their aroma, and a lime wheel.

STRAWBERRY DAIQUIRI

Fruit daiquiris got a bad rap in the 1980s and 1990s, when convenience mattered more than actually producing a tasty drink, but making a delicious fruit-flavored daiquiri is fairly straightforward. Add an approximately palm-sized amount of fruit to a classic daiquiri recipe, add some ice, and blend.

Ingredients
2 fluid ounces light rum
1 fluid ounce lime juice
1 fluid ounce Simple Syrup (see page 18)
4–6 ripe strawberries or equivalent amount of
    another fruit, plus one slice to garnish

Instructions
Combine all the ingredients in a blender. Add 1 cup of ice and blend for 20 seconds. If the mixture is too thick, add some more lime juice and Simple Syrup in equal parts. Pour into a wine glass and garnish with a sliced strawberry.

Tip: The sweetness of your base fruit matters in this drink. If your fruit is underripe or lacks the needed sweetness, don't be afraid to up the amount of Simple Syrup in the recipe.

RUMBA

David A. Embury's *The Fine Art of Mixing Drinks* is famous among bartenders both for his witty writing as well as his classic cocktail recipes. The Rumba is an Embury original, of which he once wrote, "Whoever thought up this snootful of liquid dynamite certainly liked his liquor hard!"

Ingredients
1 fluid ounce gin
1 fluid ounce white rum
1 fluid ounce lime juice
½ fluid ounce grenadine
¼ fluid ounce Simple Syrup (see page 18)

Instructions
In a cocktail shaker, combine all the ingredients with some ice and shake vigorously. Strain into a highball glass filled with crushed ice.

ZOMBIE

Donn Beach was famous for writing his cocktail recipes in a secret code so that others couldn't steal them. This version of the Zombie with rum, fruit juices, and Passionfruit Simple Syrup is likely a fairly close approximation of his original creation, although no one knows quite for sure. What is known is that there are many recipes for the Zombie and most contain a variety of fruit juices and rums mixed together. Feel free to experiment with your own combinations—just make sure to write your notes in secret code, like Donn.

Ingredients
1 fluid ounce light rum
1 fluid ounce dark rum
1 fluid ounce pineapple juice
1 fluid ounce lemon juice
1 fluid ounce lime juice
1 fluid ounce Passionfruit Simple Syrup (see page 19)
½ fluid ounce Simple Syrup (see page 18)
2 dashes of Angostura bitters
float of overproof dark rum (optional)
a mint sprig, to garnish

Instructions
Add all the ingredients except the overproof dark rum to a cocktail shaker. Add some crushed ice and shake vigorously. Strain into a highball glass filled with crushed ice. Using a bar spoon, float overproof dark rum on the surface of the drink, if you like. Garnish with a mint sprig.

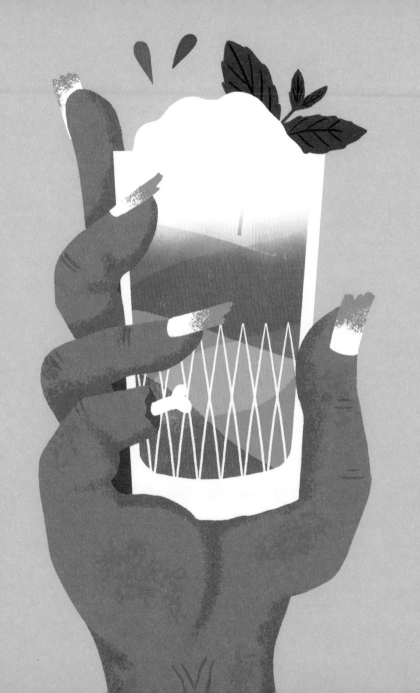

CUBA LIBRE

From a rallying cry during the Spanish-American war, Cuba Libre, meaning "Free Cuba," was created when a US Cavalry Officer added Coca-Cola to his Bacardi rum and squeezed in a bit of lime. The result was so popular that people order it by name today, even though Bacardi rum is no longer produced in Cuba and Coca-Cola is no longer sold in Cuba. This is an easy party drink; often people make substitutions, but for the classic Cuba Libre it simply must be the genuine articles—Bacardi and Coca-Cola.

Ingredients
2 fluid ounces Bacardi rum
Coca-Cola, to top up
a lime wedge

Instructions
Pour the rum into a glass and fill with ice. Top up with Coca-Cola. Squeeze the lime wedge over the drink and drop it in, then stir once to combine.

BETWEEN THE SHEETS

If you enjoy a classic Sidecar cocktail (cognac, lemon, triple sec), then meet the Between the Sheets. This risqué-sounding cocktail adds rum for a two-spirit base and eschews the traditional sugared rim for a lemon twist. For a variation of this drink with the same name, substitute gin for the rum.

Ingredients
1 fluid ounce cognac
1 fluid ounce white rum
1 fluid ounce triple sec
½ fluid ounce lemon juice
a lemon twist, to garnish

Instructions
Add all the ingredients to a cocktail shaker. Fill with ice and shake vigorously, then strain into a coupe glass. Express a lemon twist over the surface of the drink, then drop it in.

NEW ORLEANS PUNCH

Rum combines with bourbon and raspberry liqueur to pack a punch in this alcoholic take on iced tea. Use cold tea for best results, as freshly brewed hot tea will result in a lukewarm glass of disappointment.

Ingredients
1 ½ fluid ounces bourbon
1 fluid ounce gold rum
1 fluid ounce raspberry liqueur (i.e. Chambord)
1 fluid ounce lemon juice
3 fluid ounces cold black tea
a lemon wheel, to garnish

Instructions
In a cocktail shaker, combine all the ingredients with some ice and shake vigorously. Strain into a highball glass filled with crushed ice. Garnish with a lemon wheel.

PIÑA COLADA

Here is the secret to making the best Piña Colada: ice cream. That's right, one scoop of vanilla ice cream added with some coconut cream, rum, and pineapple will create the perfect backdrop for this tropical cocktail.

Ingredients

2 fluid ounces white rum
½ fluid ounce dark rum
1 scoop of vanilla ice cream
¼ ounce diced pineapple
1 fluid ounce coconut cream
1 fluid ounce pineapple juice
a pineapple wedge, to garnish

Instructions

Combine all the ingredients in a blender. Add 1 cup of ice and blend for 20 seconds. If the mixture is too thick, add more pineapple juice as needed. Pour into a hurricane glass and garnish with a pineapple wedge.

QUEEN'S PARK HOTEL, PORT OF SPAIN, TRINIDAD, B.W.I.

QUEEN'S PARK HOTEL · TRINIDAD

QUEEN'S PARK SWIZZLE

Closed in 1996, the Queen's Park Hotel in Trinidad didn't last as long as its namesake cocktail. A combination of bitters, mint, rum, and lime juice creates an eye-catching cocktail with red, yellow, and green layers if properly made. Trader Vic called this swizzle "the most delightful form of anesthesia given out today," so gather your ingredients and see for yourself.

Ingredients
10 mint leaves, plus a sprig to garnish
1 fluid ounce Simple Syrup (see page 18)
2 fluid ounces Demerara rum
1 fluid ounce lime juice
4–6 dashes of Angostura bitters
a lime wheel, to garnish

Instructions
Add the mint leaves and Simple Syrup to the bottom of your glass and muddle to release the herb's essential oils. Add the rum, lime juice, and 2 dashes of bitters and fill the glass with crushed ice. Swizzle the drink with either a swizzle stick or bar spoon just above the layer of mint, being careful not to disturb the mint on the bottom. Swizzle until frost forms on the outside of the glass. Top off with more crushed ice, molding the ice slightly above the glass. Add the final 2–4 dashes of bitters. Garnish with a mint sprig and lime wheel.

TEST PILOT

Trader Vic's Southern Californian tiki drink rival Donn Beach's motto was, "If you can't get to paradise, I'll bring it to you." This boozy blender drink is both refreshing and complex, and it's easier to make than it looks. Pour everything into a blender, add some ice, and seconds later you'll have made a bona fide delicious tiki cocktail.

Ingredients
1 ½ fluid ounces dark rum
1 fluid ounce light rum
½ fluid ounce lime juice
½ fluid ounce triple sec or Cointreau
½ fluid ounce falernum
1 dash of Angostura bitters
6 dashes of absinthe
a cherry, to garnish

Instructions
Add all the ingredients to a blender with 1 cup of ice. Blend on high for 5–10 seconds. Pour into a glass and garnish with a cherry.

JET PILOT

Created in a famous Beverly Hills celebrity hangout in the 1950s, the Jet Pilot is the best known of the variations on the Test Pilot (other riffs, including the Astronaut and the Space Pilot, have ended up being relegated to obscurity). This was the height of the tiki craze in the United States, and this nine-ingredient cocktail combines three rums, cinnamon, and citrus with absinthe and bitters to create a potent frozen concoction.

Ingredients

1 fluid ounce overproof Jamaican rum
1 fluid ounce overproof Demerara rum
¾ fluid ounce gold rum
½ fluid ounce grapefruit juice
1 fluid ounce lime juice
½ fluid ounce Cinnamon Simple Syrup (see page 19)
½ fluid ounce falernum
a dash of absinthe
a dash of Angostura bitters
a cherry, to garnish

Instructions

Add all the ingredients to a blender with 1 cup of ice. Blend for 5–10 seconds on high. Pour into a glass and garnish with a cherry.

CAIPIRINHA

Brazil's national spirit, cachaça, is made from fermented sugar cane juice, giving it an earthy and grassy flavor that mixes well when muddled with lime wedges and granulated sugar.

Ingredients
1 lime, cut into wedges
approx. 2 tsp superfine sugar
2 fluid ounces cachaça

Instructions
In a rocks glass, muddle the lime wedges and sugar together using a twisting motion. Add ice to fill, then top with the cachaça. Stir briefly to combine the ingredients.

BATIDA

The second most popular drink in Brazil, the Batida takes grassy sugar-cane-based cachaça and pairs it with coconut cream and condensed milk for a sweet, tropical frozen drink that is easy to make in batches in your blender. Traditionally served beachside in plastic cups with no garnish, we've added a playful twist with a few sprinkles of toasted coconut to add flair.

Ingredients

8 fluid ounces cachaça
1 can of sweetened condensed milk
1 can of cream of coconut (Coco Lopez or similar)
toasted coconut sprinkles, to decorate the glass or garnish

Instructions

Add all the ingredients to a blender with 1 ½ cups of ice. Blend on high for 5–10 seconds until smooth and creamy. Pour equal portions into 4 glasses and garnish each with toasted coconut sprinkles, or if you prefer you can coat the rim with the sprinkles (see page 23 and follow the method used for coating the rim of the glass with superfine sugar, substituting for sprinkles).

DR. FUNK

Absinthe in a tiki drink? While this sounds unusual, the small amount of absinthe in this drink gives structure and body to the cocktail, allowing experimentation with a variety of different rums that will all yield delicious results. Named after Robert Louis Stevenson's doctor in Samoa, who once prescribed Stevenson an absinthe-laced limeade as a restorative, the original Dr. Funk recipe was created by Donn Beach in the 1950s, although multiple variations abound now.

Ingredients

2 fluid ounces dark rum
¼ fluid ounce absinthe
12 fluid ounces lemon juice
½ fluid ounce lime juice
¼ fluid ounce grenadine
½ fluid ounce Simple Syrup (see page 18)
club soda, to top up
a mint sprig, to garnish

Instructions

In a cocktail shaker, combine all ingredients except for the club soda. Add some ice and shake vigorously for 20–30 seconds. Pour the contents of the shaker into a glass and top up with club soda, then garnish with a mint sprig.

KAVA

The Kava is an old tiki drink that is perfect for making at home. It is easy to prepare, delicious, and packs a bit of a potent punch. This is also an easy drink to make in a tiki bowl and share among friends. Fair warning—imbibe a few Kavas and you'll either be the life of the party or wearing the lampshade, or possibly even both.

Ingredients
1½ fluid ounces light rum
½ fluid ounce gold or dark rum
1 fluid ounce pineapple juice
1 fluid ounce lemon juice
½ fluid ounce Simple Syrup (see page 18)
¼ fluid ounce grenadine
a pineapple wedge speared with a cherry
    on a cocktail stick, to garnish

Instructions
In a cocktail shaker, combine all the ingredients with some ice and shake vigorously. Pour the contents of the shaker into a tiki mug. Garnish with a pineapple wedge speared with a cherry a cocktail stick.

Make it a pitcher: Increase the quantities of each ingredient by 4, and combine everything in a tiki bowl with some ice, and garnish.

BULLDOG

The Bulldog is a close cousin of the White Russian (replacing the vodka with rum and adding Coca-Cola) and the Colorado Bulldog (the same as this drink but substituting vodka for rum). All three are delicious drinks, but the Bulldog is perhaps the most interesting, with the pairing of rum and Coca-Cola mixed with coffee and cream. Easy to make, this drink is perfect for those with a bit of a sweet tooth or those who don't enjoy spirit-forward drinks.

Ingredients
2 fluid ounces white rum
½ fluid ounce kahlúa coffee liqueur
3 fluid ounces half and half
Coca-Cola, to top up

Instructions
Add the first three ingredients to a cocktail shaker with some ice and shake vigorously. Pour the contents of the shaker into a glass. Top up with Coca-Cola.

19 FLAVOURS

FALERNUM

LIQUEUR

PRODUCT OF BARBADOS

AROMATIC

BITTERS

WICKED WAHINE

Spiced rum is delicious, and yet often it doesn't get used in cocktails beyond a simple spiced rum and cola combination, but this modern riff on a rum sour base is proof that spiced rum deserves a place in your home cocktail bar. Missing fresh hibiscus flowers? Don't worry, use your imagination for an alternative garnish, or just leave them out altogether.

Ingredients
1 ½ fluid ounces spiced rum
¼ fluid ounce falernum
¼ fluid ounce lemon juice
¼ fluid ounce lime juice
¼ fluid ounce Passionfruit Simple Syrup (see page 19)
¼ fluid ounce grenadine
a dash of Peychaud's Bitters
a fresh hibiscus flower, to garnish (optional)

Instructions
In a cocktail shaker, combine all the ingredients with some ice and shake vigorously. Strain into a coupe glass and garnish with a fresh hibiscus flower, if you like.

CABLE CAR

The Starlight Room was a San Francisco cocktail bar icon for many years, sitting on top of the Sir Francis Drake Hotel. While working there, Tony Abou-Ganim (known as The Modern Mixologist) created the Cable Car as a nod to San Francisco's famous mode of transportation through the city. As a cocktail, the Cable Car takes the idea of the classic Sidecar (brandy, lemon, and orange liqueur) and swaps the brandy for spiced rum. This was an instant success at the Starlight Room and remains one of the best spiced rum cocktails ever created. Make sure not to forget the cinnamon-sugar-spiced rim on this one, as it takes the drink to another level.

Ingredients
a lemon wedge
cinnamon and sugar mix, for decorating the glass
½ fluid ounce spiced rum
¾ fluid ounce orange curaçao
1 fluid ounce lemon juice
½ fluid ounce Simple Syrup (see page 18)

Instructions
Coat the rim of a glass by running a lemon wedge around it, then dip the wet glass into a shallow dish with the cinnamon sugar. Add all the remaining ingredients to a cocktail shaker with some ice and shake vigorously. Strain into a coupe or martini glass.

FISH HOUSE PUNCH

It's hard to imagine that a fishing club in the late 1700s concocted this potent punch to kick off meetings, but that is exactly what the Schuylkill Fishing Company in colonial Philadelphia did. It's unknown whether any members actually caught fish after imbibing this punch, but this drink is still a great option for parties or holiday gatherings. This recipe will yield approximately 80 fluid ounces, so break out the punch bowl or make this in a pitcher for sharing.

Ingredients
8 fluid ounces Simple Syrup (see page 18)
28 fluid ounces black tea (at room temperature)
8 fluid ounces fresh lemon juice (lime works, too)
1 bottle (750ml or 700ml) gold or dark rum
12 fluid ounces brandy
2 fluid ounces peach brandy
lemon wheels, to garnish

Instructions
Combine all the ingredients in a punch bowl or a pitcher. Stir briefly to combine. Add some ice (an ice block is a nice touch in a punch bowl but not essential), garnish with some lemon wheels and use a ladle to serve.

SCORPION

The Scorpion is a tiki drink that has more variations than perhaps any other tiki drink. Often, bartenders will just mix up fruit juices with a rum or two (or three), then perhaps add a float of grenadine and, lacking a name for their concoction, will simply label it a Scorpion. This recipe, however, traces back to Trader Vic himself, so while it isn't the only Scorpion recipe, it is the most authentic. This is a great option for parties and cookouts, and feel free to get creative with the garnishes in your punch bowl.

Ingredients

1 bottle (750ml or 700ml) gold or dark rum
½ bottle white wine (think pinot gris or sauvignon blanc)
2 fluid ounces gin
2 fluid ounces brandy
8 fluid ounces orange juice
8 fluid ounces orgeat syrup
2 large sprigs of mint
citrus slices and edible flowers, to garnish

Instructions

Combine all the ingredients except the mint in a punch bowl or pitcher. Crush the mint between your hands to release the herb's oils before adding to the other ingredients. Stir briefly to combine. Let sit for 2 hours for the flavors to marry—do not skip this step. Add ice (an ice block is a nice touch in a punch bowl but not essential), garnish with some citrus slices and edible flowers, and use a ladle to serve.

SCORPION

SAUVIGNON BLANC

2020

FRESH
ORANGE
JUICE

BACARDI COCKTAIL

One wouldn't think that the United States Supreme Court would get too involved in cocktail recipes, but in 1936 it did just that. The Supremes ruled that in order to be called a Bacardi Cocktail, the drink must be made with Bacardi rum. Bacardi Superior white is usually used in this cocktail, but feel free to substitute any Bacardi rum for a nice twist. This variation on the Daiquiri features Bacardi rum with lime juice and grenadine to create a delightful pink-colored drink.

Ingredients
2 fluid ounces Bacardi rum
1 fluid ounce lime juice
1 fluid ounce grenadine

Instructions
In a cocktail shaker, combine all the ingredients. Add some ice and shake vigorously for 20–30 seconds. Pour the contents of the shaker into a chilled glass.

BLUE HAWAII

Hawaii's most famous cocktail creation is the Blue Hawaii, created at the Kaiser Hawaiian Village (now the Hilton Hawaiian Village Waikiki) by legendary bartender Harry Yee. A combination of blue curaçao, rum, vodka, lime juice, and Simple Syrup mixed with pineapple juice, this drink is as visually striking as it is tasty.

Ingredients
1 fluid ounce vodka
1 fluid ounce white rum
½ fluid ounce blue curaçao
3 fluid ounces pineapple juice
½ fluid ounce lime juice
½ fluid ounce Simple Syrup (see page 18)
a pineapple wedge speared with a cherry
    on a cocktail stick, to garnish

Instructions
Add all the ingredients to a cocktail shaker. Fill it with ice and shake vigorously. Strain into a hurricane glass filled with pebble ice, and garnish with a pineapple wedge speared with a cherry on a cocktail stick.

DARK 'N' STORMY

One of Bermuda's most famous drinks that features its own Goslings Black Seal rum, the Dark 'N' Stormy has been a registered trademark of Goslings since 1991. While some people may change the name and substitute another rum, nothing quite compares to Black Seal rum in this cocktail and, trademark or no trademark, substituting it just simply makes it fall short of the mark.

Ingredients
2 fluid ounces Goslings Black Seal rum
ginger beer, to top up
a lime wedge, to garnish

Instructions
Pour the rum into a highball glass filled with ice. Top up with ginger beer and stir lightly with a spoon to combine. Garnish with a lime wedge.

BEACHCOMBER

This variation on the classic Daiquiri features both triple sec and maraschino liqueurs, so it should be sweet enough, but if you need a bit more sweetness in this drink don't hesitate to add ½ ounce of Simple Syrup. Try this one on the rocks for a different serve if you find the up version too stiff—the addition of extra ice helps water down the drink's alcohol punch a bit.

Ingredients

2 fluid ounces white rum
½ fluid ounce triple sec
1 fluid ounce lime juice
¼ fluid ounce maraschino liqueur
a pineapple wedge speared with a cherry
    on a cocktail stick, to garnish

Instructions

Add all the ingredients to a cocktail shaker. Fill with ice and shake vigorously. Strain into a martini glass or coupe and garnish with a pineapple wedge speared with a cherry on a cocktail stick.

FOG CUTTER

"Fog Cutter? Hell, after two of these things you won't even see the stuff"—Trader Vic, 1947. While this rum-based tiki drink often gets denigrated as the tiki version of a Long Island Iced Tea, a properly made Fog Cutter is both potent and much better tasting than a Long Island. While many give Trader Vic credit for this drink, there are several others who claim to have created the Fog Cutter as well. Regardless of who created the drink, the result is both potent and complex. For a Nordic variation, substitute aquavit as a float instead of cream sherry.

Ingredients

2 fluid ounces white rum
1 fluid ounce brandy
½ fluid ounce gin
2 fluid ounces lemon juice
1 fluid ounce orange juice
½ fluid ounce orgeat syrup
float of cream sherry
a mint sprig, to garnish

Instructions

Add all the ingredients (except the cream sherry float) to a cocktail shaker. Fill with ice and shake vigorously, then strain into an ice-filled ceramic tiki mug or a hurricane glass. Float cream sherry on top of the drink by slowly pouring it over the back of a bar spoon. Garnish with a mint sprig.

EL FLORIDITA DAIQUIRI

Named after the El Floridita Bar in Havana where bartenders still blend these all day for hordes of customers thirsty to try this cocktail in the home of the Daiquiri. While the El Floridita blends their own version (and you are certainly welcome to blend your own, just add 1 cup of ice to the ingredients in your blender), this shaken version is a bit more flavorful and elegant.

Ingredients
2 fluid ounces white rum
1 fluid ounce lime juice
¼ fluid ounce maraschino liqueur
¼ fluid ounce Simple Syrup (see page 18)
a lime wheel, to garnish

Instructions
Add all the ingredients to a cocktail shaker. Fill with ice and shake vigorously, then strain into a martini glass or coupe. Garnish with a lime wheel.

JACK

DEMPSEY

JACK DEMPSEY

The Manassa Mauler, boxer Jack Dempsey, knocked out 53 of his 70 opponents in his world-championship career. Cold and bracing, his namesake cocktail is a combination of white rum and gin cut with just the slightest amount of lemon and sugar. This cocktail will help to take the edge off, but it also packs an alcoholic punch. This isn't a drink for the fainthearted but if you enjoy a stiff drink you'll enjoy adding this one to your repertoire.

Ingredients
1 ½ fluid ounces white rum
1 ½ fluid ounces gin
¼ fluid ounce lemon juice
¼ fluid ounce Simple Syrup (see page 18)
a cherry, to garnish

Instructions
Add all the ingredients to a cocktail shaker. Fill with ice and shake vigorously, then strain into a martini glass or coupe. Garnish with a cherry.

MARY PICKFORD

Mary Pickford, the 1920s' film actress, lends her name to this sweet but subtly potent cocktail. Legend has it that Pickford and husband Douglas Fairbanks were in Havana, Cuba, working on a film when this drink was created for her by a local bartender. While the origin of this drink might be 100 or so years old, this classic cocktail remains as modern as ever and is a great place to kick off one's enjoyment of rum cocktails.

Ingredients

2 fluid ounces white rum
2 fluid ounces pineapple juice
¼ fluid ounce grenadine
⅛ fluid ounce maraschino liqueur

Instructions

Add all the ingredients to a cocktail shaker, fill with ice and shake vigorously. Strain into a martini glass or coupe.

MAYHEW'S WORLD'S BEST HOT BUTTERED RUM

This is literally the best recipe for hot buttered rum you'll ever find. Even better, it's easy to make and eminently adaptable. Can't find agave syrup? Substitute another liquid sugar like maple syrup. Out of cloves? It won't be quite as good but you'll be OK. Someone in your party doesn't drink? This is great even without any alcohol, although the addition of a tea bag in its place adds a bit more pizzazz than just pouring hot water over the batter. The batter keeps well when frozen, so make a large batch and use as needed.

Ingredients
2 fluid ounces rum
1 spoonful Buttered Rum Batter (see below)

Instructions
Add the rum and batter to a coffee mug or Irish coffee glass and top up with hot water. Stir until the batter dissolves and incorporates.

Buttered Rum Batter: Stir together 1 stick butter (at room temperature), ¾ cup brown sugar, ¼ cup agave syrup, ½ tsp ground cinnamon, ⅛ tsp grated nutmeg, ⅛ tsp ground allspice, ⅛ tsp ground cloves, and a pinch of salt until combined. Cover and keep refrigerated until ready to use. Or store for up to 3 months in a sealed container in the refrigerator or freezer.

TOM & JERRY

An old-fashioned holiday drink dating from the 1820s, the Tom & Jerry is a strong, spiced winter warmer. While the batter takes a bit of work, the reward of being able to enjoy a proper Tom & Jerry makes it well worth it.

Ingredients

1 fluid ounce dark rum
1 fluid ounce brandy
1 spoonful Tom & Jerry Batter (see below)
hot whole milk, to top up
grated nutmeg and ground cinnamon, to garnish

Instructions

Add the rum, brandy, and batter to a coffee mug or Irish coffee glass and top up with hot milk. Stir until the batter dissolves and incorporates. Serve sprinkled with grated nutmeg and ground cinnamon.

Tom & Jerry Batter: Separate 4 eggs; whip the egg whites in a nonreactive bowl with ¼ tsp cream of tartar until it reaches stiff peaks. In a separate bowl, beat the yolks with 1 cup of superfine sugar, ½ fluid ounce dark rum, and ¼ tsp vanilla extract. Once the yolk mixture is done, fold the yolks gently into the egg whites. Cover and keep refrigerated until ready to use. Or store for up to 3 months in a sealed container in the refrigerator or freezer.

PLANTER'S PUNCH

Planter's Punch is one of the classic rum drinks. Drinks historians debate where the Planter's Punch was first created, with cities such as Charleston and St. Louis often mentioned, but the most likely place for this to have been created is Jamaica. This drink is such a staple there that for many years the Jamaican rum brand Myers put the Planter's Punch recipe right on its bottle.

Ingredients
3 fluid ounces dark rum
1 fluid ounce Simple Syrup (see page 18)
1 fluid ounce lime juice
¼ fluid ounce grenadine
2–3 dashes of Angostura bitters
splash of club soda
a mint sprig, to garnish

Instructions
Add all the ingredients except the club soda to a cocktail shaker. Fill with ice and shake vigorously. Strain into an ice-filled collins glass. Top off with a splash of club soda and garnish with a mint sprig.

CARIBBEAN COFFEE

Rum pairs incredibly well with coffee, and in this winter warmer the addition of amaretto adds just enough sweetness to create a drink that will both satisfy your sweet tooth and warm you from the inside out.

Ingredients
2 fluid ounces gold or dark rum
1 fluid ounce amaretto
freshly brewed hot black coffee
whipped cream
ground cinnamon and grated nutmeg, to garnish

Instructions
Add the rum and amaretto to a coffee mug or Irish coffee glass. Fill with hot coffee and top with the whipped cream. Serve sprinkled with ground cinnamon and grated nutmeg.

WELCOME TO THE CARIBBEAN

GUN CLUB PUNCH #1

Toward the end of Trader Vic's life he published the recipe for his Gun Club Punch #1 and even specified that it should be served in a green ceramic mug resembling a shotgun cartridge. This current version has been modernized a bit, and while a tiki mug would work very well for this presentation, so would a collins glass.

Ingredients
1 fluid ounce white rum
1 fluid ounce gold or dark rum
¼ fluid ounce orange curaçao
¼ fluid ounce grenadine syrup
¼ fluid ounce Simple Syrup (see page 18)
2 fluid ounces pineapple juice
1 fluid ounce lime juice
a mint sprig and mixed fruit (think pineapple wedge
    with an orange wheel and cherry), to garnish

Instructions
Add all the ingredients to a cocktail shaker, add some ice, and shake vigorously. Strain into an ice-filled tiki mug or collins glass. Garnish with a mint sprig and as much fruit as you can fit into the glass.

EL PRESIDENTE

Cuba was a popular vacation destination for Americans during the Prohibition era, and the El Presidente was created during that time to honor Cuba's president. The El Presidente cocktail is a fun drink to play around with. A gold or dark rum will yield a richer, full-bodied cocktail, and dialing up or back on the vermouth and curaçao are also interesting ways to tweak this recipe to your own tastes.

Ingredients

2 fluid ounces white rum
1 fluid ounce dry vermouth
½ fluid ounce orange curaçao
⅛ fluid ounce grenadine

Instructions

Add all the ingredients to a cocktail shaker. Fill with ice and shake vigorously, then strain into a martini glass or coupe.

ALEXANDRA

The Alexandra packs quite a punch behind two full ounces of navy-strength rum (50% ABV) and coffee liqueur, but it's also an eminently quaffable sipper. Best as an after-dinner drink, the Alexandra will have you ready to take on the next round in wherever the evening's adventures take you.

Ingredients
2 fluid ounces navy-strength rum
1 fluid ounce coffee liqueur
1 fluid ounce half and half
grated nutmeg, to garnish

Instructions
Add all the ingredients to a cocktail shaker with some ice and shake vigorously. Strain into a martini glass or coupe. Garnish with grated nutmeg.

ALAMAGOOZLUM COCKTAIL

While the origins of the Alamagoozlum Cocktail are murky at best, it's John Pierpont Morgan, better known as J.P. Morgan, who popularized this drink. As fun to say as it is to drink, the Alamagoozlum gets harder and harder to pronounce after each consecutive drink you consume.

Ingredients
1 fluid ounce dark rum
¾ fluid ounce genever
½ fluid ounce yellow chartreuse
⅛ fluid ounce orange curaçao
4 dashes of Angostura bitters
¼ fluid ounce Simple Syrup (see page 18)
a cherry, to garnish

Instructions
Add all the ingredients to a cocktail shaker. Fill with ice and shake vigorously. Strain into a martini glass or coupe and garnish with a cherry.

NAVY GROG

Not to be confused with the grog served to the enlisted ranks in the British Navy, which was a combination of rum cut down with water and perhaps some citrus to prevent scurvy, this Navy Grog was created by Donn Beach. Featuring 3 kinds of rum, 2 juices, and honey, this is the kind of drink that sailors could only dream about when on their ships.

Ingredients
1 fluid ounce dark rum
1 fluid ounce Demerara rum
1 fluid ounce white rum
1 fluid ounce Honey Simple Syrup (see page 19)
½ fluid ounce club soda
½ fluid ounce grapefruit juice
½ fluid ounce lime juice
a lime wheel and mint sprigs, to garnish

Instructions
Add all the ingredients to a cocktail shaker. Fill with ice and shake vigorously. Strain into an ice-filled double rocks glass and garnish with a lime wheel and mint sprigs.

CORN 'N' OIL

Why does a drink that contains neither corn nor oil get called a Corn 'N' Oil? Well, the best guess is that the blackstrap rum looks like oil as it winds its way through the other ingredients. As for the corn, that remains a mystery for the ages. Perhaps the original incarnation of this drink was garnished with baby corn until someone finally thought better of it and dropped it, but by then the name had stuck. Or not…

Ingredients
2 fluid ounces blackstrap rum
½ fluid ounce falernum
½ fluid ounce lime juice
4 dashes of Angostura bitters
a lime wedge, to garnish

Instructions
Fill a double rocks glass with ice and pour in all the ingredients. Stir to combine and garnish with a lime wedge.

GOLDEN WAVE

Created in 1969 in California, this frozen blender drink is easy to make and hard to mess up. Light, fruity, and refreshing, this is the perfect frozen drink for backyard parties and summer days.

Ingredients

2 fluid ounces white rum
½ fluid ounce triple sec
½ fluid ounce falernum
1 fluid ounce pineapple juice
¾ fluid ounce lime juice
a pineapple wedge speared with a cherry
    on a cocktail stick, to garnish

Instructions

Fill a blender with all the ingredients and one cube of ice. Blend on frappe or high for 30 seconds until smooth (add more pineapple juice if needed). Pour into a hurricane glass and garnish with a pineapple wedge speared with a cherry on a cocktail stick.

GOLDEN RETRIEVER

Dick Bradsell was an influential bartender, who played an important part in reviving the cocktail scene in London in the 1980s. Credited as the creator of the original Espresso Martini, with the Golden Retriever Bradsell puts gold rum up against an intriguing combination of green chartreuse and Licor 43.

Ingredients
1 fluid ounce gold rum
1 fluid ounce green chartreuse
1 fluid ounce Licor 43
an orange twist, to garnish

Instructions
Add all the ingredients to a cocktail shaker. Fill with ice and shake vigorously. Strain into a martini glass or coupe and garnish with an orange twist.

PANCHO VILLA

Before the Philippines had Manny Pacquiao as their boxing hero, there was Francisco Villaruel Guilledo. This Filipino flyweight boxing champ was nicknamed "Pancho Villa," and this cocktail was created in his honor and published in 1939.

Ingredients
1 ½ fluid ounces white rum
1 fluid ounce gin
½ fluid ounce apricot liqueur
½ fluid ounce pineapple juice
¼ fluid ounce Cherry Heering
¼ fluid ounce lime juice
a cherry, to garnish

Instructions
Add all the ingredients to a cocktail shaker, fill with ice, and shake vigorously. Strain into a martini glass or coupe. Garnish with a cherry.

FLAMING DR PEPPER

You may have heard the saying that God protects fools and drunkards, but that doesn't apply to the Flaming Dr Pepper. This flaming shot of overproof rum and amaretto dropped into a lager beer may be reminiscent of Tom Cruise in *Cocktail*, but use extreme caution any time you flame alcohol. Interestingly enough, it really does taste like Dr Pepper as it goes down and it puts on quite the show as the flaming shot glass is dropped into the beer.

Ingredients
8 fluid ounces lager beer
1 fluid ounce amaretto
½ fluid ounce 151 proof or overproof rum

Instructions
Fill a 16-ounce pint glass halfway with beer. Add the amaretto to a shot glass and top with the rum. Using a match or lighter, ignite the rum and then carefully drop the flaming shot glass into the pint of beer.

INDEX

CREDITS

Lance J. Mayhew would like to thank:

Amelia, Samuel, and Charlotte, I'm so proud of each of you and being your father is the greatest gift I've ever received. Life is a great adventure, take advantage of it. Raena, you truly are my better half. Wayne and Denise Downer, thank you for everything. Mom and Dad, I love you. Christie Mayhew, I light a candle for you wherever I travel. You are always in my heart. Richard DellaPenna and Joseph "Moose" Morante, two of my bartending mentors who we lost too soon. Chris Curtis at Sacramento's Club2Me, one of the great bartenders in America. Mike Dunne and Jeff Lindell, thanks for being such great friends. Jason and Grace Thornton, you are amazing people. Steve Mendiola, one of the greatest people I've ever met. Paul and Manda Hardy, thank you for your friendship and sense of humor. Terry Boyd, Brian Shannon, Matt Wilcox, great people who make radio seem easy. Maybe too easy. John Zimmer and Jennifer Moore, thank you. Rand and Rachel Harris, thanks for your great friendship. And, finally, thank you to Caitlin Doyle and Sarah Varrow, the two finest editors anywhere. I'm lucky to work with you.